to Tania

Thank you for your help and friendship
on the long creative path.

Thank you to Ted Jnr and John
for translation permission and assistance on page 23

For further information about the Gamilaraay and Yuwaalaraay languages go to: yuwaalaraay.com
A wide range of Gamilaraay and Yuwaalaraay resources are available as free downloads,
and others can be purchased from: www.fivesenseseducation.com.au

First published in 2019 by Windy Hollow Books
PO Box 265, Kew East, Victoria, Australia 3102
www.windyhollowbooks.com.au
www.facebook.com/windyhollowbooks

ISBN: 9781922081773 (hardback)
Reprinted 2020

Design by Nuovo Group. Printed in China.

A catalogue record for this book is available from the National Library of Australia

Dreaming of Australia A to Z

By Jess Racklyeft

A is for Australia,
that
great southern land,

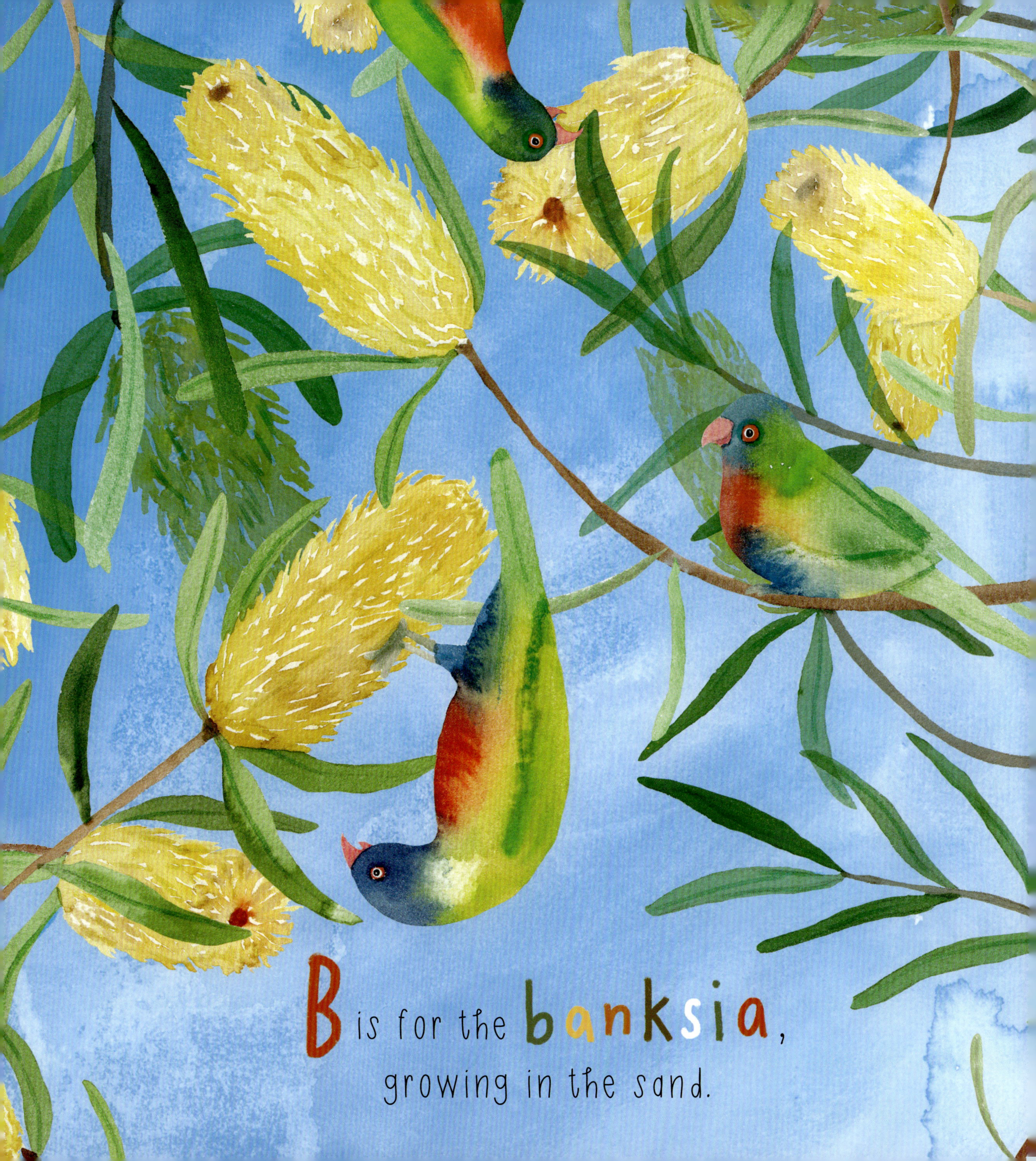

B is for the banksia,
growing in the sand.

C for the cockatoos, screeching through the sky,

D is for the dingo,

snapping at the flies.

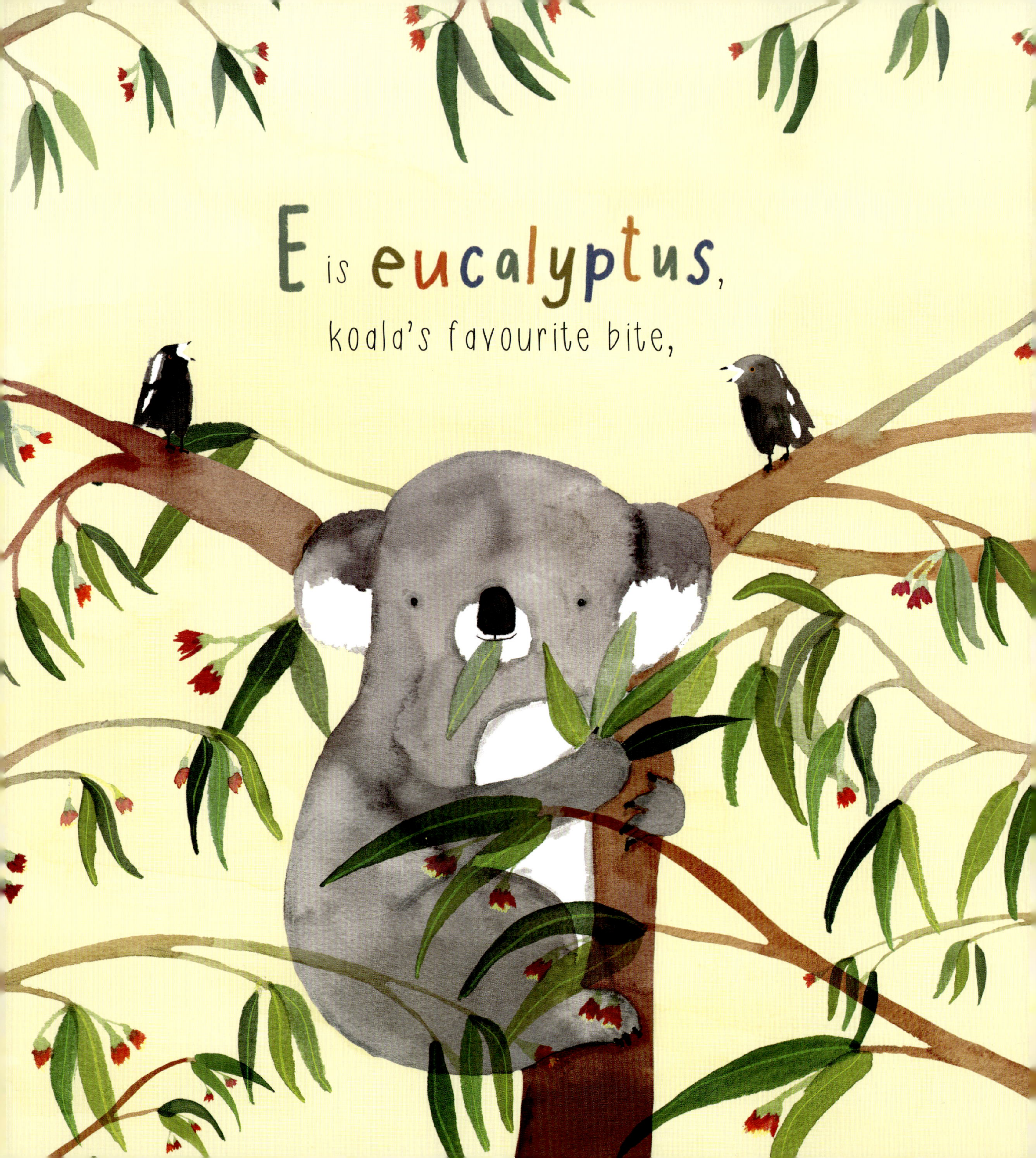
E is eucalyptus,
koala's favourite bite,

F for the fairywren,

tiny blue delight.

G is a goanna,

resting from a run,

H the spiked hakea,

thriving in the sun.

I is for this island,

ringed by ocean deep,

J for a Jillaroo,
rounding up the sheep.

Let's take a kip in Kakadu,
and rest our head on K

Now the heat is breaking,
and we can finish off our day.

Country Womens Association
L – the lamingtons,
for our afternoon tea,

M – the macadamia,
from the wild tree.

N – the hungry **numbat**,
searching for termites,

O for many
great owls,
hooting through
the night.

P is for the picnic, in a park in Perth,

Q is for the quokka,

digging up the earth.

R is for the rain,
the farmers hope to see,

S is a sugar glider, flying over me.

T for tassie devils,

growling in the night,

U – huge Uluru –
the sacred sandstone site.

V is for Vegemite,
spread thick on your bread,
W is for
wattle,
tickling at
your head.

X is for

a town in W.A.,

Y – "yaluu maliyaa" –

"goodbye mate" you say.

Z is the tired echidna,
settling down to bed,

Softly curling up those spikes,

dreaming of
A to Z.